HOPPER THE HOOT
HAS A HOLIDAY

Small actions make **BIG** difference.

Love Planet Earth...

...and Reduce, Reuse and Recycle.

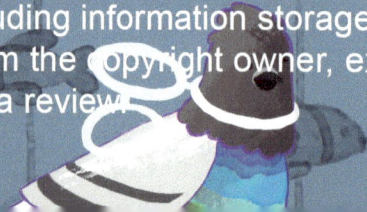

HOPPER THE HOOT
HAS A HOLIDAY

Paridhi P Apte

Hopper the Hoot is going on a
HOLIDAY.

Hopper flies across the valley, through the dense forest and over the big city until he reaches the beach.

Oh, what a **WONDERFUL** day!

Time to relax after such a long journey.

5

Waves lap the shore
and seagulls **SWOOP** and **CRY.**

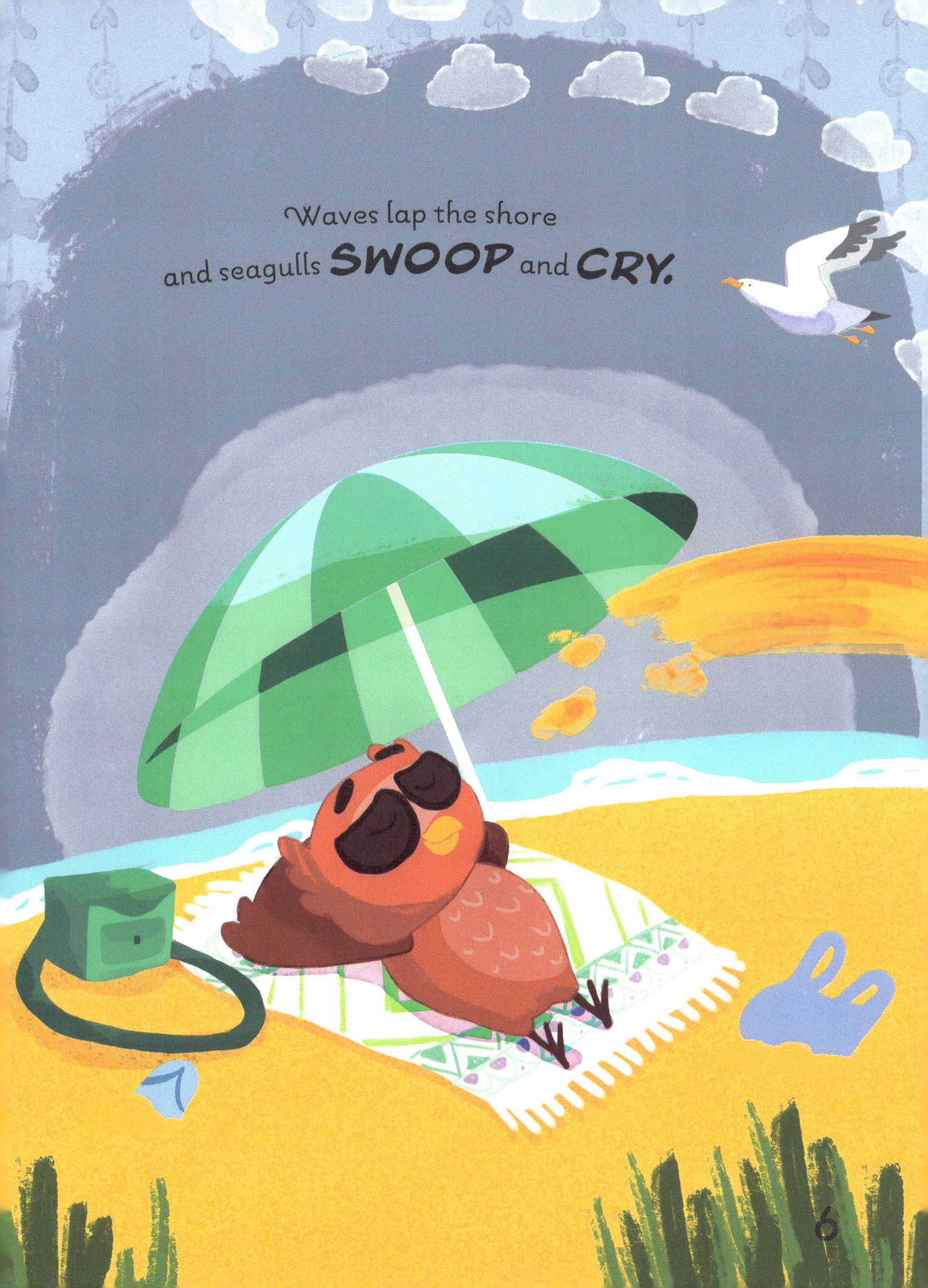

Suddenly, sand and rubbish rains on Hopper.
HE JUMPS UP ANGRILY.

boink

OH NO!
Denzel is making a sandcastle nearby.

"OI! WOULD YOU QUIT DOING THAT?" asks Hopper. "Can't you see I am trying to enjoy my quiet day at the beach?"

Oi!

"OH, I AM SORRY," says Denzel.
"I didn't mean to disturb you.
I am just building a sandcastle."

Would you like to
join me?

Together we could build a
BIGGER castle.
Wouldn't that be
GREAT!

MILK

I would simply like to have a peaceful nap."

"NO THANK YOU!

Hopper humphs.

Denzel gives a friendly smile.
"Come on, buddy, it would be fun!
We can make a **GINORMOUS CASTLE,**
the **BIGGEST** the world has ever seen."

Hopper likes that idea.
He can tell his friends at home he made a
**SUPER AWESOME
GINORMOUS
MEGA CASTLE.**

**"SURE,
LET'S DO IT,"**

he says.

16

TOGETHER THEY DIG
AND DIG
AND DIG...

oh my!

UH-OH!

There is a huge pile of rubbish
alongside their sandcastle.

"HOW DID ALL THIS RUBBISH GET HERE?" asks Hopper.

"It looks like no one bothered to use the garbage
bins while they were enjoying the beach."

Denzel sighs.
"THIS IS A DISASTER.
With all this rubbish around,
our sandcastle will not look any good.
We will have to clean up the rubbish
to make the beach beautiful again."

"Yes," says Hopper. "BUT WE WILL NEED HELP."

20

"Mr Seagull, will you help us clean up the beach?" asks Hopper.
"WHY SHOULD WE?" squawks Mr Seagull.
"We didn't make the mess!"
"NO," agrees Hopper. "But if we work together and help
each other we can clean up the mess swiftly and enjoy
this beautiful beach sooner."

"All right, my friends and I would help,
but on one condition." says Mr Seagull.
**"YOU WILL HAVE TO REWARD US
LATER WITH SOME FISH. DEAL?"**
Hopper hesitates, but agrees.

22

Meanwhile, Denzel approaches the echidna
who's sunbathing nearby.
"Hello, Mr Echidna, Hopper and I are cleaning up the beach.
Will you help us pick up the empty plastic bottles?"

"I come here often but lately it's been awfully
unpleasant," says Eddie the echidna. "I would
rather go and find a new clean beach than
spending time cleaning this one."

23

"You can do that, Mr Echidna, but I am sure that all the beaches nearby would be much like this one," says Denzel.

"Our oceans are **FILLED WITH RUBBISH** that enters from the rivers, and the ocean tides dump all the rubbish back to the seashore."

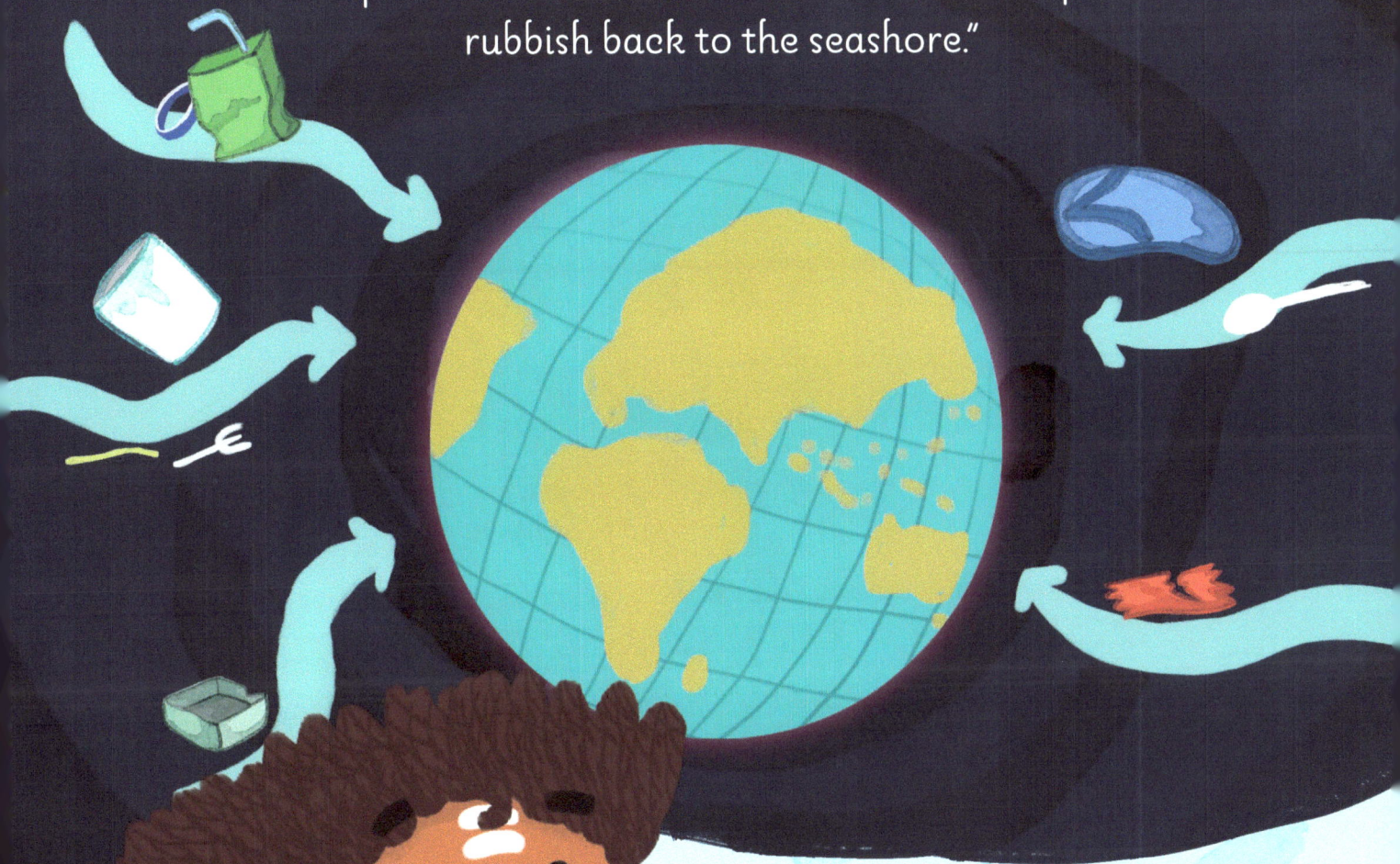

"I never thought about it like that. Of course, I will help you to clean up the beach."

Across the shore, Hopper asks the crabs if they will help remove the **PLASTIC RINGS** stuck in the sand?

"Good day mate,
I'm glad you asked," says Kirby.

"Me and my friends have had a hard time
finding shells lately.
We often end up making the **EMPTY
CARTONS** our temporary homes. We will be
happy to help you clean up the beach."

Hopper, Denzel, the seagulls, Mr Echidna and all the crabs work hard to clean up the beach.

MANY garbage bags later,
the beach is slowly being restored to its glory.

"The beach looks so much better now," says Hopper.
"GREAT JOB EVERYONE!

We all must be careful how we dispose of our rubbish.

It is essential to make sure **RECYCLABLE ITEMS** are placed in the correct bins. Otherwise, they will end up in landfill and get into our ocean from the rivers.

29

If we use the wrong bins, our rubbish can be dumped back onto our beaches by the ocean tides."

Hopper finally gets to enjoy his holiday. He has also made some new friends and they have all learned to be mindful about how they dispose of their garbage.

Together they have built a sandcastle
that is just the **RIGHT SIZE.**

No, he did not forget to reward
Mr Seagull and his friends with fresh fish.

AFTER ALL, SOME OWLS
ARE EXPERT AT FISHING!

People who visit the beach and leave their litter behind is not the only reason why some beaches are filled with rubbish.

Most of the rubbish or plastic that is found on the beach is from the ocean. Our oceans are filled with plastic that enters from the rivers.

This plastic in the ocean not only harms the sea life, but also affects us as it enters our food chain through sea salt and sea food.

We should be mindful of:

• using correct bins for different kinds of rubbish
• recycling as much as we can
• reducing the consumption of plastic altogether

All of this will help us to reduce ocean rubbish pollution.
(source: theoceancleanup.com)

Find the following throughout the book
and write down the page number in the box next to it.

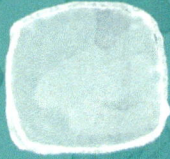

X 2 Bar-tailed
Godwit birds

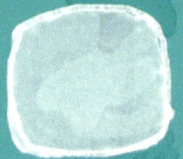

X 5 Fish picture
frames

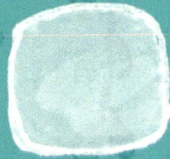

X 1 Crab
with treasure map

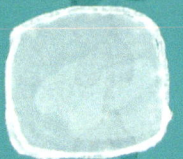

X 1 Snorkeling
giraffe

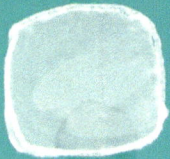

X 1 Rooster
with surfboard

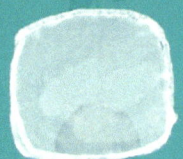

X 1 Helping turtle

X 1 Polar bear with
heart shaped nose

X 1 Crab
with sea shell

COLOR
Hopper and friends

www.ingramcontent.com/pod-product-compliance
Lightning Source LLC
Chambersburg PA
CBHW060825270326
41931CB00002B/68